SO YOU HAVE A CHILD WITH AUTISM IN YOUR CLASSROOM!!! NOW WHAT?

Dr. Teri Baldwin
So You Have a Child With Autism in Your Classroom!!! Now What?

Published by Spines
ISBN: 979-8-89383-774-2

SO YOU HAVE A CHILD WITH AUTISM IN YOUR CLASSROOM!!! NOW WHAT?

A TEACHER'S GUIDE TO GETTING PREPARED!

DR. TERI BALDWIN

CONTENTS

Introduction   ix

1. What Is Autism?   1
2. Accommodations   12
3. The Iep Team   19
4. Room Set Up   30
5. Visual Supports   35
6. Rules   38
7. Behavior   42
8. People First Language   47
9. Talking To Parents   50

Afterword   59

(Read this guide over the weekend; you should be much more prepared.)

INTRODUCTION

Your day starts something like this....

"You're giving me a boy with what? I already have 30 kids in my classroom!"

"You're moving 2 kids to another teacher?" *Great, that will make all the difference! Shoot, I didn't say that out loud did I? Mmmm. Doesn't seem like it. Whew…….. I could quit and be a Walmart greeter, they always seem so pleasant. I can say, "Hi, welcome to Walmart."*

"I'm sorry, what did you say?" " Oh, he will have a paraprofessional with him sometimes?"

Sometimes?? I hope she knows what to do because I sure don't!

"But I'm not a special education teacher! I don't know how to teach kids with special needs! Oh, the special ed teacher will consult with me, that's good." *I can't freaking believe this! Who is the special ed teacher again? How do I find her? Or is it him?*

"Isn't he the boy with the parent that always calls and has those really long IEP meetings?"

I don't even know what an IEP is. How will I pick up my daughter after school if I have all of those long meetings? Quick… think! What else could I do? I could tutor. But that won't pay enough. I could be a flight attendant and travel… but the kids.

"What? Yes, I'm ok.*" Don't cry! Don't cry! Don't cry! Deep breath."*

"Of course, I'll make this work. Thank you, have a good afternoon."

Thank you, ugh! That's like telling a police officer thanks for the ticket and have a nice day."

This is a Shit Hit the Fan, Shit Just Got Real scenario!

"They could have told me at the beginning of the summer so I could have prepared. I could have taken a class or gone to a training or something. Shit! Fu@#! Oh, I really need to stop cursing… fudge nuggets! Hmm, that works."

"I'm going to run to the bookstore and see if there is some kind of book that can help me… but I have to be able to read it over the weekend! Kids start Monday."

Well, here is your book…

WHAT IS AUTISM?

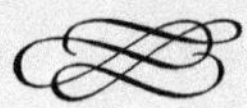

Autism is first and foremost a label that attempts to describe difficulties or challenges that a person on the spectrum may face. When a teacher can fully understand the learning differences between a neurotypical and neurodivergent (autistim) child, they can teach more beneficially and comprehensively. Autism is considered a combination of deficits in language, social skills, and mental flexibility. It affects how students interact with others, learn, communicate, and behave. It is considered a neurological and developmental syndrome that requires years of speech therapy, occupational therapy, and behavioral therapy.

Really, how about in layman's terms?

The "official" definition from the Center for Disease Control and Prevention cites, 'Autism spectrum disorder is a developmental disability caused by differences in the brain.' Let's take this one step at a time. First, a "spectrum disorder" means there are a wide variety of cognitive impairments. The spectrum ranges from nonverbal students and students with severe cognitive impairments all the way to those with high IQs who are hyperlexic and experts in certain topics. Next, let's cover the "disorder" part. Autism Spectrum Disorder is basically a communication and social disorder. This means the social skills of a child are always delayed by at least three years. Did I say always? Yes, I did… but that's just in my 30 years of experience.

The biggest obstacle is, that no two kids with Autism are the same. What works for one student, may not work for another. What works today, may not work tomorrow. But, once you understand how the child learns, it might help you punt when you need to and it will help you be prepared. ***I can punt. I do it every time the darn projector won't turn on.*** For example, a student with autism kept calling out in class even though we had a positive behavior system in place. I wrote "Be quiet, raise your hand, and wait until you're called on" on a sticky note and it worked. Another time I was introducing the reading assignment and the student on the spectrum started to get upset so I pivoted and let him choose a book on trains which was his passion and he immediately calmed down.

COGNITIVE SKILLS

Children on the Autism spectrum *often* display extensive knowledge in one or two areas and are uninterested in anything else. You need to find out what those areas of interest are!!! More often than not, for young children, these interests include Legos, Minecraft, trains, video games, particular movies, or characters. For older children, things like computers, war, and Star Wars may spark their interest. So start there. Inquire about what their interests are. This is how you can establish rapport. You need to talk to the child about his area of interest. If you do not do that, **you** will not matter to the student. When you discuss the area of interest, you become important; you become part of that world that they find interesting. I go out and buy anything to do with that subject (stickers, books, toys, etc.) and either use them as a reward or use them academically. But we will talk more about academics later.

Organizing and Planning

Typically, the student will have poor problem-solving and organizational skills. They may do the homework, but it's wadded in the bottom of their backpack or in the wrong folder. Helping them organize their folders and backpacks may become your job if the parent doesn't do it for them. I like to use different colored paper with corresponding colored folders to make things easier for them and for me. For example, the science folder is yellow and I print the homework on yellow paper or put a yellow stripe on top with a highlighter if I am short on time. See example in Figure 1. Other examples may be helping them to fill out their planner and sign/stamp it, using technology when possible such as posting assignments on your website so they have something to fall back on if the paper gets lost, or emailing the parent or student the assignment. A good tool for all students is for you to post a weekly calendar on the board with objectives and assignments. Don't get hung up on making them copy the assignment down. They can take a picture with their phone.

Figure 1: *Color Coded Class Periods*

Note: *Lau, B., (2018).* Using color to organize the secondary classroom. *Science with Mrs. Lau. https://www. scienceandmathwithmrslau.com/2016/09/using-color-stay-organized-secondary-classroom/*

Organizing and planning are usually areas of great difficulty for students on the autism spectrum. Graphic organizers as shown in Figure 2 can be used as prompts for students with autism to create their ideas, organize and sequence material, and compare and contrast information presented (Llynch, 2021). There are many kinds of graphic organizers such as Venn diagrams, topic webs, T charts, main idea and supporting details, and story webs. Relational organizers (Figure 1) can support the demonstration of reasoning, judgment, and the connections between facts and supporting concepts (Llynch, 2021).

Figure 2: *Examples of Relational Graphic Organizers*

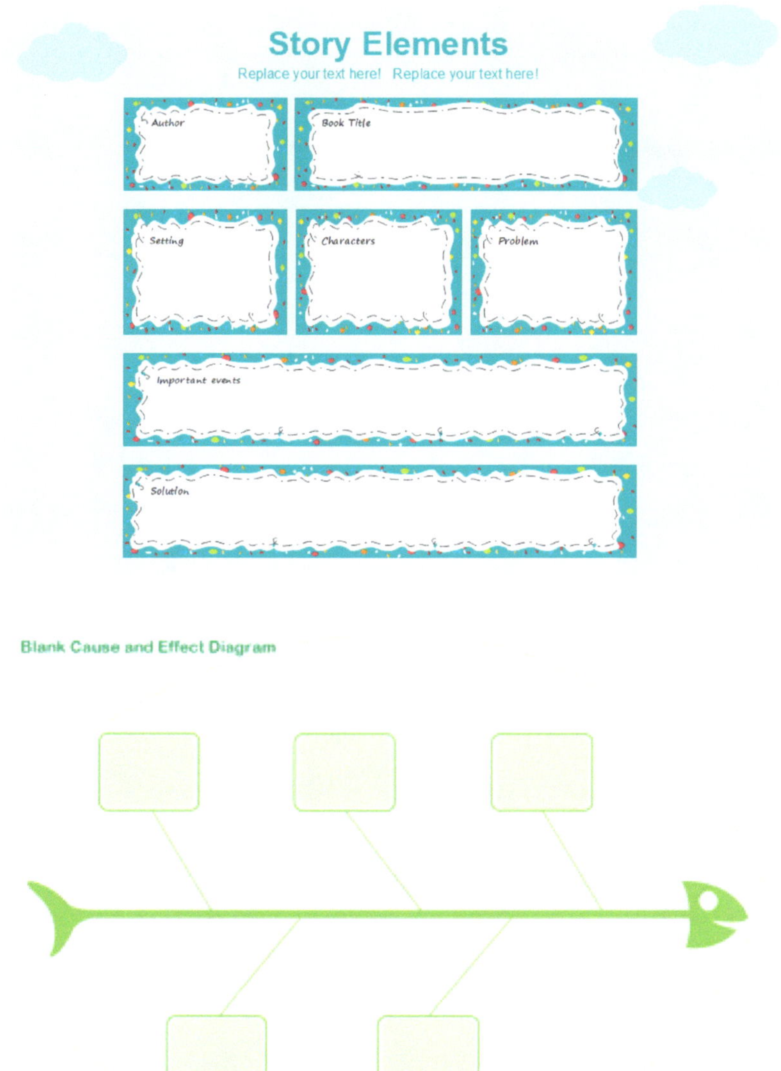

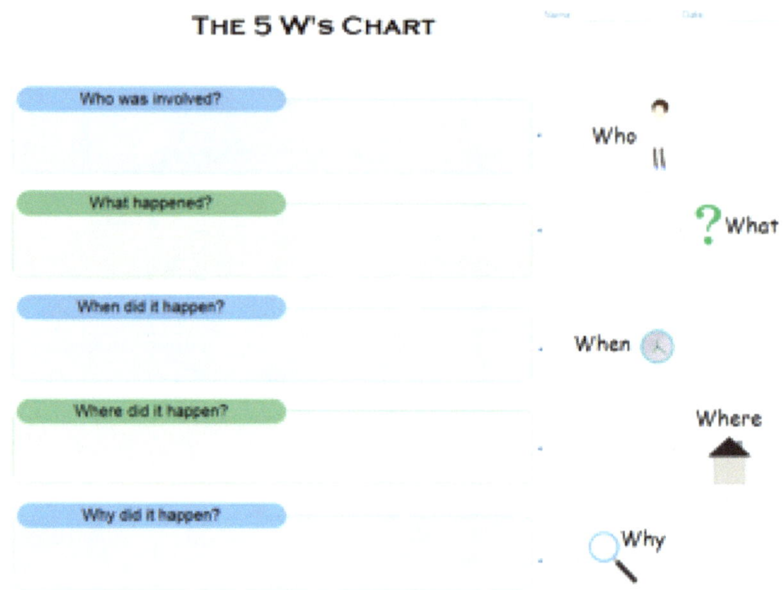

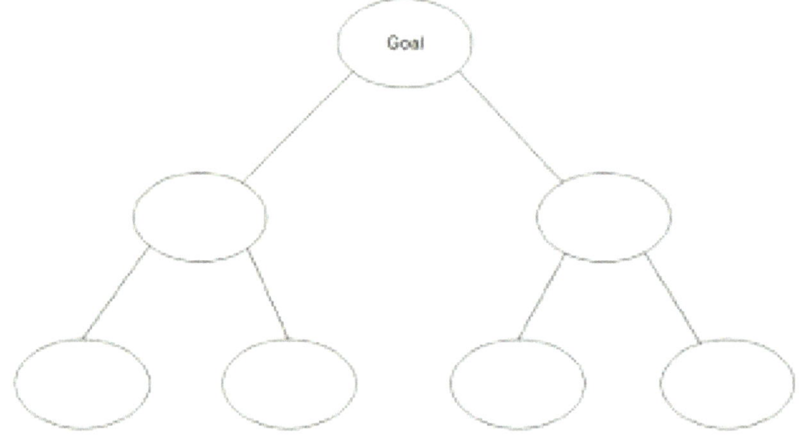

Note. *Wondershare edraw. (n.d.).* What Is a Graphic Organizer? *[Photograph].*
https://www.edrawsoft.com/what-is-graphic-organizer.html.

Executive Functioning Skills

Students with autism have cognitive strengths and weaknesses, just as their typically developing peers do. The somewhat universal weaknesses associated with autism usually involve a lack of theory of mind (students not being able to predict their peers' and parents' thoughts and feelings), poor executive functioning skills, and difficulty with behavior regulation and control (Pellicano, 2010). These cognitive deficits end up having a significant impact on academic skills and social skills.

The student will most likely display a lack of executive functioning skills, see Figure 3, which is a lack of cognitive control including:

- attention
- impulse control
- emotional control
- cognitive flexibility
- reasoning
- task initiation
- organizing
- planning

Note that you don't have to have Autism to have executive functioning difficulties. This issue leads to **very literal thinking**. They take everything literally, so do not use figurative language (similes, metaphors, exaggerations, alliterations, sarcasm) such as, "She's as happy as a clam, It's raining cats and dogs, You look like an angel, You are a beast." Students with Autism do not get sarcasm, so don't use it. (If you have not experienced this before, start watching Big Bang Theory, Sheldon is a great example of a rigid and literal thinker).

Figure 3: *Executive Functioning Skills Overview*

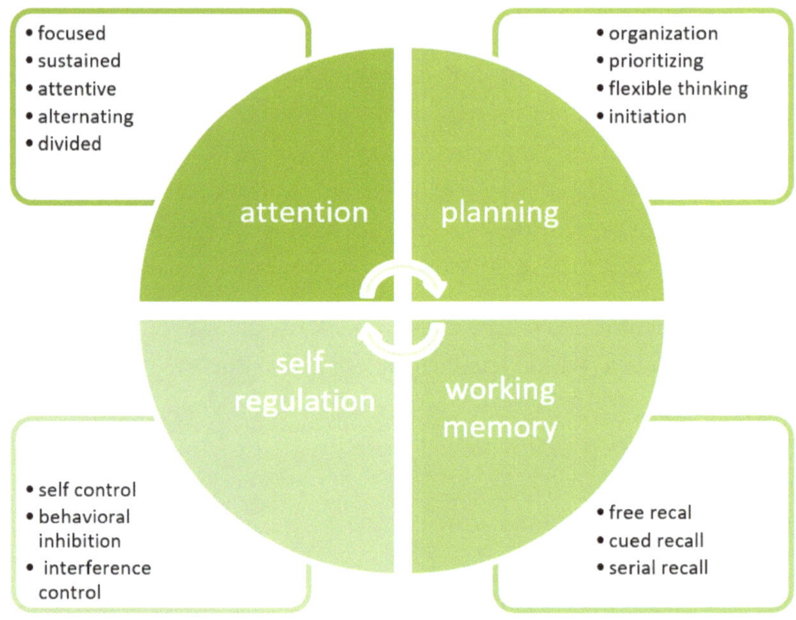

The students with ASD also have a hard time understanding how their behavior affects others, which leads to them not being manipulative, even if you think they are. They appear very self-centered and only care about what they want to do and their topics of interest. So, you have to establish rapport… you have to!

Discussing the student's favorite topics is the perfect way to establish rapport with students with ASD. I cannot emphasize this enough. Teachers who share an interest in the topic become important to the student with ASD. The topic can be used as a reinforcer in the classroom. A potential dialog could be "First you complete your math assignment, then you can have 5 minutes with the train toys." The teacher can use favorite topics, such as trains, to put train stickers on math papers to make them exciting or assign a book report on the history of trains. The teacher should use the students' intense interest to their advantage to engage the students whenever possible.

Bring in their topics whenever you can. You may let them talk about their topic for three minutes at the beginning of the day. Add stickers to your worksheets so their favorite character is on the worksheet. Let them read books about their interest and broaden it from there. There are all kinds of ways to incorporate their favorite topic into the day.

SOCIAL SKILLS

The student with ASD will be socially much younger or more immature than their peers. In your classroom, this student may make a lot of off-topic or negative comments, such as "A train can go 120 miles an hour," "This is stupid" or "boring." They do not know what is relevant to the current topic you are teaching. Or, if he is only interested in his narrow topics, everything else IS boring or stupid. Don't be alarmed, but he may call you stupid, too. (I'm just preparing you! Don't panic… we can fix this!)

Other times the child will withdraw into their own narrow world, and replay movies in his head, laugh at the funny parts, and even say familiar lines out loud. At the very least, the verbal student will correct you often or tell you ACTUALLY it's like this. The words "actually" and "boring" have become the bane of my existence. A lot of kids on the spectrum perseverate on a particular topic or question. They may ask you about it all day. For the nonverbal student, he may get up and laugh and rock. He may flap his hands. He may tap and shake items.

Conversation Skills

For most neurotypical students, conversational skills have developed organically and effortlessly. They unconsciously use their body to convey messages and maintain eye contact when having conversations, discussions, and even arguments.

Conversely, students on the spectrum may find conversations very difficult. Difficulties initiating and maintaining conversations often exclude them from developing friendships and impede their school participation. Students with autism typically communicate to get their wants and needs met or to discuss favorite topics, rather than to socialize, comment on their environment, or build relationships.

SENSORY SKILLS

Sensory Challenges in layman's terms are symptoms that may affect the senses, such as hearing, touch, or taste. It often affects multiple senses. Students can be under or over-responsive to stimuli. Body awareness can be affected and so can movement, balance, and coordination. According to the Child Mind Institute, http://childmind.org/article/how-sensory-processing-issues-affect-kids-in-school/

Overly sensitive students will *avoid* stimulation:

- Have trouble tolerating bright lights (like when you have a headache or migraine),
- Be overwhelmed by loud noises like fire drills, or chairs scraping on tile,
- Avoid clothing that is scratchy, tight, or has tags,
- Avoid shoes because they are tight,
- Avoid touching or hugs, even from Mom,
- Avoid swings and playground equipment,
- Have trouble knowing where their body is in space, and in relation to other people; appear clumsy.
- Run away when situations are too stressful or overwhelming,
- Have trouble sensing the amount of force they're using when writing or erasing,

Students who are under-sensitive will often *seek out more* stimulation. They can:

- Have an extremely high tolerance for pain,
- Have trouble sitting still,
- Not giving personal space or having a constant need to touch people or textures,
- Not understanding their own strength
- Have a strong need to jump or crash into things.
- Crave deep pressure, wrestling, and strong hugs,
- Love spinning, and swinging movements.

All of these issues can make it extremely challenging for the student to focus and attend lectures, activities, homework, conversations, and tasks.

Since each child is different, each child might have a different accommodation.

Well crap, where do I find their accommodations??

Let's look at that right now, in Chapter 2.

ACCOMMODATIONS

The boring but necessary conversation starts with The Individuals with Disabilities Education Act (IDEA), which is a federal law that requires schools to serve the educational needs of eligible students with disabilities. This means that every child with a disability has a right to attend general education classes and to have accommodations and modifications so they can be successful in those classes. These can include changes in the method of instruction, the curriculum, and the environment.

The very first thing you need to do is read the accommodation page of the IEP before school starts before the child walks into your classroom. In fact, read the goals and present levels too. *The parent expects you to provide the accommodations on the first day of school and by law, you need to.* The first day sets the tone and establishes the rules that the student may follow going forward, so you really do need to be ready. Once you get a copy of the accommodations, it won't take you more than five minutes to read them. Accommodations may be a change in your delivery of instruction (using simple sentences, using an FM system, adding pictures into your lecture), or the method of student performance (only completing the odd-numbered problems, not rewriting the question in his answer, extra time to do homework assignments.) An accommodation does not change the content of the curriculum. Other common classroom accommodations include preferential seating (front of the room, seated next to a helpful student), and things you would have done anyway.

Examples are as follows:

Instruction accommodations:

- Provide visual supports (schedules Figure 4, first-then strips Figure 5, checklists Figure 6, directions)

Figure 4: *Visual Schedules*

Note: *Shanahan, A. (2023).* How to set up a self-contained classroom. *Simply Special Ed.https://www.simplyspecialed.com/how-to-setup-a-self-contained-classroom/*

Figure 5: *First-Then Board*

Figure 6: *Symbol Schedule for Washing Hands*

Note: *Symbol schedule made with Mayer-Johnson symbols.*

- Limit spoken language when presenting directions (keep directions short and to the point i.e. "Open book to page 200").

- Use reinforcements (token board, stickers, candy)
- Limit distractions in the classroom (e.g., number of posters on the walls)
- Pair verbal directions with visual support such as pointing or pictures.
- Provide social stories
- Provide social support at recess and lunch
- Provide an organizational system
- Provide assistive technology (low- to high-tech)
- Use manipulatives (Figure 7)

Figure 7: *Example of Cheerio Manipulatives to Count*

Note: *Teaching Tiny Tots (n.d.).* Cheerio counting. *https://www.teaching-tiny-tots.com/toddler-math-cheerio-count.html*

- Allow use of fidgets (Figure 8)

Figure 8: *Frog Fidget*

- Allow flexible seating Figure 9 (wobble stool, standing, rocker)

Figure 9: *Alternative Flexible Seating*

- Provide access to a calming corner or sensory room
- Provide extra breaks and movement

- Schedule movement breaks
- Allow extended processing time
- Provide a sentence or paragraph starters
- Provide a self-editing checklist
- Provide lists to support writing or math work (transition word list, math operations word list)
- Provide access to noise-canceling headphones
- Allow the use of a calculator on math assignments
- Reduce homework assignments
- Provide textbooks and materials for at-home use
- Provide a study carrel
- Provide extra visual or verbal cues and prompts

Testing Accommodations:

- Allow responses to be recorded in a test booklet
- Frequent breaks (every 10 minutes, for example)
- Extend allotted time (by 60 minutes or double the time permitted for the test)
- Untimed testing
- Test in a separate location
- Testing in small groups (less than 10 students)
- Testing in a one-on-one setting
- Administer the test in several sessions or across several days
- Allow students to take sub-tests in different orders
- Administer a test at a specific time of day
- Provide extra paper or space for writing
- Allow choice of test format where applicable
- Allow open-book or open-note tests
- Highlight key directions
- Provide a study guide before the test
- Read tests or read directions aloud to the student
- Preview test procedures
- Rephrase or simplify test wording and/or directions

The two biggest mistakes that I see teachers make are putting the child in the back of the room (where they can see all 29 desks, backpacks, pencils, water bottles, and children talking or tapping their pencils) and then not calling on them or not including them in the class. If a student is nonverbal, you can ask them a yes/no question. They can answer, shake their head, or hold up a yes/no sign. *But what if he's wrong? I don't want to put him on the spot and make him feel bad.* So what if their answer is wrong? Other students give the wrong answer. If they are often wrong, I may give them only the yes sign and ask questions where the answer is yes. It's important to build a sense of community in your classroom and not ostracize the student. *What teacher would do something like that?* More than you think. When they don't know how to include the student, or the student is disruptive and they don't know why or how to calm the student, they often stick the child in the back of the room with a paraprofessional or ask them to go next door in the empty classroom next door to work.

Okay, so where do these accommodations come from? Do the parents make them up? Is that my responsibility?

The accommodations are designed by the previous IEP team. I can tell you with great certainty that to put together the individualized education plan (IEP) it took at LEAST five hours combined from all of the team members, plus an hour or two at the meeting with the parent to develop the IEP and to determine which accommodations are necessary. So don't take the accommodations lightly, a lot of work went into establishing them. The accommodations are what you are bound by law to provide, the goals typically fall on the shoulders of the rest of the team. Let's meet your team…

"I have a team?"

THE IEP TEAM

Yes, you do… well, the student has a team and you are part of that team. The special education staff can support you. The special education teacher is often the team leader and is responsible for the academic goals. The goals will be worked on either in the classroom, (yes your classroom) or in the special education room. The previous team has already decided which is best, so there is no point in arguing about either decision. Special education teachers are some of my favorite people in the whole world. I know you are overworked. ***Damn right, I am. I spend all weekend grading homework and tests and planning.*** I know! My daughter is a high school math teacher. What I want you to know is that the special ed teacher often does not get prep and often eats their lunch with their students. They are almost always overworked and dealing with angry parents, IEPs, multiple therapists, and a variety of teachers which tends to burn them out by October.

You might think that the special education teacher knows everything there is about Autism, but that is often very untrue. A lot of times, the special education teacher has only had students with learning disabilities or has only worked in a self-contained environment. He or she may have only worked with three students at a time and has never had to "push in" to deliver services in the general education room.

ADAPTING THE CURRICULUM

The special education teacher is responsible for adapting the curriculum. This is true, but in my experience, the special education teacher often has an unmanageable caseload; they have to provide goals to students from all grades, write IEPs, deal with parents, and train paraprofessionals. As a result, they are not given time to adapt the curriculum for all of their students. Legally, it is the teacher's responsibility and the paraprofessional is not allowed to adapt the curriculum. Adapting the curriculum you are teaching may fall to you. Chances are, you already have a lower academic group of students that you are spending extra time with or making things easier for them to understand. It's basically differentiated instruction. ***But how do I differentiate enough?***

One thing I try to do is to make it easier and meet the student's needs. Stay with the topic a little longer. Use the same book all week or all month. Add fidgets and sensory boxes such as in Figure 10 to the unit. For example, if you are teaching life cycles, let the student hold a frog fidget as in Figure 11. Use models and manipulatives such as in Figure 11. Anything hands-on often works.

Figure 10: *Gardening Sensory Bin*

Figure 11: *3D Model of Plant Life Cycle*

TECHNICAL INDIVIDUALIZED EDUCATION PLAN INFORMATION

There are many legal timelines involved in the IEP process. After the initial referral, the IEP team must meet within 15 school days to discuss the concerns and what evaluations are needed. This scenario includes the speech therapist, administrator, parents, and general education teacher. The team is not concerned about Jacob's academic learning abilities, so the special education teacher is not involved. The group discusses their concerns and decides if testing is necessary to determine if the student requires special education services, specifically speech therapy. The team determines they need testing to determine if the student qualifies for special education. This meeting is called a PRE-MET (pre-multidisciplinary evaluation team meeting). The team has 45 days to complete testing and hold an eligibility meeting. This meeting is called the MET (multidisciplinary evaluation team meeting). The results of the testing are discussed, and the team determines, based on the testing scores, if Jacob qualifies for special education services under speech and language impairment. Jacob scored below normal limits for expressive language and articulation and did qualify for special education services with a speech and language impairment. When a student qualifies for special education, the IEP team reconvenes within 30 calendar days to create the IEP (goals and supports needed).

The IEP is prepared by the special education teacher or speech-language pathologist, and on rare occasions, the physical therapist who coordinates the input from the general education teachers, and school nurse if applicable. There are several required components of the IEP. The present levels of (educational) performance are a required section (IDEA, 2017). It is a segment of information describing the student's current academic performance and areas of concern. This section also explains how the student's disability affects their progress and participation in the general education curriculum and discusses related areas such as social skills, motor skills, and behavior (Logsdon, 2022). In this continued scenario, Jacob is at grade level for math, but his unintelligibility and poor expressive language skills are interfering with successful reading and writing (below grade level), as well as his ability to socialize with peers and work in a group. Goals are formed from the weaknesses listed in the present levels of performance. The IEP is reviewed annually, and the evaluation is reviewed every three years.

The entire IEP team (parents, administrators, special and general education teachers, and therapists) is responsible for providing FAPE to special education students by providing accommodations, adaptations, and modifications. Although the entire team is responsible, there are individual roles. Predictably it depends on who oversees the IEP, sometimes called the case manager or support coordinator, which can be the special education teacher, the speech-language pathologist, or a physical therapist (not as common). *Occupational therapy is not a standalone service and cannot be provided unless it is a related service.* Some special education students are "pulled out" of the general education classroom for reading, writing and/or math, speech, occupational therapy, physical therapy, and/or nursing services, depending on what they qualify for on their IEP. Other students remain in the general classroom with variable accommodations that meet the needs of their specific disability and /or receive "push-in" services, where the special education teacher comes into the classroom or team-teaches with the general education teacher.

The speech-language pathologist (SLP) is responsible for:

- articulation (sound development),
- expressive language skills
- receptive language skills

- fluency (stuttering)
- voice (hoarseness, breathiness)
- pragmatics (social skills).
- AAC augmentative alternative communication such as talking devices or pictures Figures 10 and 11.

Figure 12: *AAC device: NovaChat*

Note: *Saltillo (n.d.).* NovaChat 5. *[Photograph]. https://saltillo.com/products*

Figure 13: *Hierarchy of AAC Devices from Low Tech to High Tech*

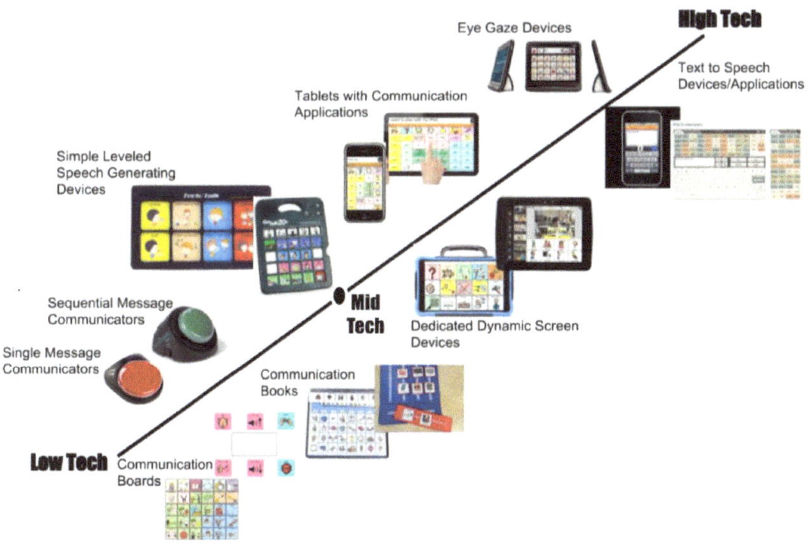

Note: *Northern Suburban Special Education District. (n.d.).* AAC continuum. *[PDF]. https://sites.google.com/a/nssed.org/nssedintegratedtech/resources/ communication/aac-continuum*

Most states do not have a minimum or maximum caseload. The average caseload size is between 50 and 75 students. That's over 50 IEPs and IEP meetings. (Arkansas has a caseload max of 45. Speech therapists should move there!) When it comes to your student on the spectrum, the speech-language pathologist can help the student with his social skills (which are always delayed), understanding the language presented, and expressing themselves appropriately. They often see the child at lunch or in the playground to work on social skills. If the student is nonverbal or has limited verbal skills, the SLP will help to develop a method for the child to communicate. They will also help you train the para to support your student with their communication skills. The student may need pictures, symbols, a computer, or an alternative augmentative communication (AAC) device. They may set rules for the student as to when they can call out and when they need to raise their hand. The child may have difficulty recognizing the feelings and thoughts of others, have poor eye contact, difficulty maintaining personal space by physically intruding on others, and have difficulty joining a group. The speech therapist works on all of those things. The SLP can work on avoiding meltdowns, helping them to understand the classroom rules, and implementing more visual supports into your classroom. If you're lucky, your speech therapist will be an Autism expert and your new best friend.

How can I ask politely if she is an Autism expert?

You can say "Have you had much experience with students with Autism?

When students reach Jr. High and High School, directions become much more complex and abstract. Think about the lectures that are given in history or social studies classes. Students with Autism start having different communication issues.

They struggle to fit in because they are unaware or don't care about what's in style, or what's age-appropriate. For example, kids may spend a lot of time talking about My Little Pony and wear My Little Pony shirts to school. They "actually" (I can't believe I said that) call themselves Bronies. Students on the spectrum typically struggle to join a group at lunch or understand when other students are mocking them or making fun of them. Students on the spectrum are often very naïve (those social skills that are years behind, really come into play here in high school) and other students learn they can trick them into doing things they shouldn't.

The Occupational Therapist (OT) addresses sensory processing issues as well as fine and gross motor issues. They can be your new best friend. The OT's caseload size doesn't usually exceed 50. The OT often works on:

- handwriting
- keyboarding
- dressing
- sensory processing
- supporting academics
- accessing playground
- self-care
- activities of daily living
- transitioning
- fine motor skills (i.e. opening containers)

The OT can address self-stimming behaviors such as rocking and flapping the hands, calling out, meltdowns, etc. The OTs are important because sensory processing issues are difficult to understand. Your student may respond in an unusual manner to sounds (e.g. ignores sounds or overreacts to sudden, unexpected noises, high-pitched continuous sounds, like the fluorescent lights buzzing). The fire alarm may hurt their ears so much that they scream, cry, and often live in terror of it going off again. An accommodation is often made so that the student is prepared and warned of an upcoming fire alarm, provided with headphones if they want them, or will leave class early to avoid the blaring alarm noise.

Sometimes the student with ASD resists or refuses activities that involve writing and they write slowly or very sloppily. That's often due to low tone and poor motor coordination. Look for an alternative if handwriting is a huge issue. They can use a keyboard or computer and type their work. He could use a marker or a special grip on the pencil. He can complete his assignment on an iPad. Your OT can help you figure out how to make handwriting easier for him. Writing activities are often the catalyst for meltdowns throughout the school day.

This leads us to the child may respond in an unusual way to pain (e.g. either overreacting to the slightest bump or tap or being completely unaware of an illness or serious injury). They may respond unusually to food (e.g. resist certain textures, flavors, and colors.) It is not unusual to see a school-age child only eating crackers, cookies, chicken nuggets, or all-orange things such as Cheetos and Doritos. The student may respond unusually to light or color (e.g. focuses on shiny items, shadows, reflections, shows preference or strong dislike for certain colors). They may need to have a yellow chair or bulletin board items may need to be stapled in all four corners so they don't flap when the AC comes on. They may respond to temperature changes or have an overreaction to smells. It's often best to avoid putting on too much perfume or strong-smelling lotion. Your student may seek out activities that provide pressure, or movement (e.g. swinging, hugging, pacing). When this happens the student usually needs this movement at the time. The OT will help you build this time and these activities into the child's schedule. Other students on the spectrum avoid activities that provide touch, pressure, or movement (e.g. resist wearing certain types of clothing, strongly dislike being dirty or messy, does not like hugs or touches). Many students make noises such as humming or singing frequently throughout the school day.

I can tell you from experience the special ed part of the team will either be your best friends or they will avoid you like the plague. The truth is that, although the special education team members have high caseloads, the OT and SLP sometimes have flexible caseloads. This means that they can help you in times of need; they can help you adapt the curriculum and help you deal with the behaviors that are sure to come. We will talk more about behaviors later because I don't want to freak you out too much at this point. ***Too late… consider me freaked out already!***

SCHOOL THERAPISTS

Often the therapists eat at their desks while they are working on reports, billing, or IEPs. They don't feel part of the school, and if they go to the lunch room, the cliques are hard to breach. Therapists get stuck trying to schedule their students *after* school has started. They will often come into your room while you are teaching or at lunch to try and schedule students. When you greet them and include them in your classroom, they will instantly like you. If you make them comfortable and welcome in your room, they will often spend more time in your room. Which means more help for you. If you are having a potluck with other teachers, invite the therapists. Typically what happens to the therapist, is that they go into a classroom and the teacher will say, "I'm teaching right now and you are interrupting," or the teacher ignores the therapist completely, like they aren't standing there, even at lunch. If you make it awkward and uncomfortable, you instantly will be the teacher to avoid. The best teachers, as far as therapists are concerned, are the ones who are flexible with scheduling and are NICE to them. That's it. Nice. Seriously! (Maybe making cookies for them and welcoming them into your room would be really nice). Ok, I know you don't have time to make gluten-free peanut-free cookies.

ROOM SET UP

What? Room setup? I've already set up my room! It's ok. Find a seat with the least amount of distractions. Look from the perspective of each seat at all of the possible distractions. Possible distractions include:

- bulletin boards
- buzzing lights
- talking students
- tapping pencils
- scraping chairs
- too much to look at
- noise from hall
- a fish tank or hamster cage
- windows

Often you won't want to sit the child near an interesting bulletin board, a window, a class pet, or by the door to the hallway. If a student needs a desk facing a plain wall to complete assignments, then he needs it. That's ok. You can have another seat for him during class discussions and lectures. When you rearrange the room or change seating, let the child with ASD keep their desk in the exact same spot. If you need to move his seat, then provide him with a written note or story explaining that he is going to move his seat on Monday. No surprises! He has to be prepared. Provide the student with a copy of the classroom rules either in pictures or words; such as you have to raise your hand to be called on, and you may not always be called on, or if you have to use the rest room just sign out and go. Whatever rules you have in your classroom need to be written out and enforced consistently.

If a child is severely affected by Autism, he will need **clear boundaries**, maybe the desk between two bookshelves and a taped square on the floor. Compare this organized classroom in Figure 14 with the over-decorated classroom in Figure 15

Figure 14: *Organized Classroom*

Note: *Gillihan, J. (n.d.)* Classroom organization and setup. *Pinterest.* *[Photograph].https://www.pinterest.com/pin/133701301313000080/*

Figure 15: *Organized Overstimulating Classroom*

Note: *CM School Supply (n.d.)* Schoolgirl style just teaches the environment. *Pinterest. [Photograph].h ttps://classborder.com/products/school-girl-style-just-teach-classroom-environment*

ELEMENTARY CLASSROOMS

If you have students sit in a big group on the floor, have a taped square or carpet square for him to sit on. In a younger elementary classroom, each area of the classroom should be clearly, and visually defined through the arrangement of your furniture (bookcases, dividers, desks, file cabinets, rugs). Each center should be defined and labeled (writing center, computer center, reading area). You do not want wide spaces where the child can run back and forth; the clearly defined centers will help the child stay in that center.

When possible, the teacher should establish clear, physical boundaries for students with ASD. For example, the teacher can use furniture to create boundaries between centers, as shown in Figure 16. Signs can be posted in each area. For example, the tape can section an area, or the teacher can place a large square of tape around the student's desk so that the student knows they can walk around inside the tape boundary. Rules for each area should be reviewed and posted for everyone in the class.

Figure 16: *Use of Furniture for Clear Physical Boundaries*

Note: *Gillihan, J., (n.d.)* Classroom organization and setup. *Pinterest.*
[Photograph].https://www.pinterest.com/pin/133701301313000080/

SECONDARY CLASSROOMS

The space where the student is allowed to go needs to be clearly defined. If the cabinet or your desk is off-limits, make that clear. Junior high and high school teachers should set up the classroom to reflect the students' age and not have circle time carpets and decorations appropriate for young children. Wall space and bulletin boards should be set up to maximize instructions for visual learners. Computers, calculators, and adapted material should be readily accessible, and all materials labeled and organized. In a resource room with multiple subjects being taught, center areas can be set up for each subject. Figure 17 shows a progressive age-appropriate center. When teaching only one subject, such as math, the classroom can be decorated, and bulletin boards created around a math theme. The teacher may want a small group table in addition to separate desks for the students.

Figure 17: *High School Resource Center*

Note: *School Outfitters (2023)*. Middle/high school resource room. *https://www.schooloutfitters.com/room/resource-room-middle-highschool*

VISUAL SUPPORTS

Have classroom structure and a routine. A consistent classroom routine and consistent classroom rules allow the student to be much more comfortable. Provide a schedule for the student, either a personal or a classroom schedule. Remember that Autism is a communication disorder. Avoid long explanations and directions. Cut right to the chase. " Do problems 1-4." "Sit in your seat." When you can take the oral language out of something, then do it. Write down directions for him, even if it needs to be in pictures because the student doesn't read yet.

Most students on the spectrum are visual learners (not all, but most). Their thoughts can be more like movies or videos. Temple Grandon is a person with autism who has written several books on her insight. She describes learning a language in pictures first, with words coming after that. This leads to processing information visually. By the same token, don't make the child look at you when you are teaching. Some children are mono-channeled and can only hear or look… so pick one. All of the facial expressions and movements can be overwhelming to a student who doesn't know what it means when you cross your arms and furrow your eyebrows.

One of the most important pieces of advice I can give you is that there are three questions that must be answered for the child on the spectrum when he is presented with "work" (or what we like to say in the sped world as a non-preferred task).

1. What is the work he has to do?
2. How much work does he have to do?
3. What is the next activity?

Let's look at each one of these. They are **extremely important**. Clear, obvious answers to these questions will avoid meltdowns over completing assignments.

1. **What is the work?** The student should be able to look at the task and know what needs to be done. If the task involves long explanations, then you may need to modify the task. So ask yourself, *can I look at this and see what needs to be done?* For example, when you look at an 8-piece puzzle, with the pieces to the side, you instantly know you are supposed to put the pieces together on the puzzle board. Examples are in Figure 18. If you are presenting a lot of information, you can do it in chunks. One piece at a time. First, read this story, then answer these three questions. On the top is the example math problem underneath are two math problems to be completed.
2. **How much work is there?** Many, many meltdowns come from the child thinking he has to do too much hard, boring work. If you give him a workbook, he may panic and think he has to do the whole book. Just give him one page of the workbook at a time. Maybe even cut that page in half. If it's math work, highlight the problems he really needs to do and cross out or hide the ones he can skip. It needs to be crystal clear how much work he has to do. You cannot say, "Well we do the same thing every day" or "I give all of the kids their

workbook." We are looking to avoid overwhelming the student and causing a meltdown. Trust me! It is far easier to avoid a meltdown than it is to calm the student down as he is having one. So, do not give him one worksheet and, when he's completed that, pull out another one. He needs to know upfront how much there is, so he knows when he is finished. Always be sure to give the student an amount of work that he can finish. Many students meltdown over not being able to finish a project. They expected to finish and can not break away from not finishing it. Remember that.

3. **What's next?** When a student with ASD does not know what's going to happen next it causes a great deal of anxiety for them. Think about it… that's why watching the same movie over and over is so much fun for him, he knows what's going to happen, what's going to come next. It's predictable. I almost always allow a reward time after the work is finished. The reward could be anything, 10 minutes on the computer, 5 minutes with a comic book, 5 minutes in the science center. I always put a time limit on the reward. Setting a timer so it dings and the student knows that the time is up……but…..they need to know what's after that, too. Is it lunch? PE? Art? Storytime? The next class? ***I get it, make a schedule!***

Prepare the student for changes. If there is an assembly let them know there will be an assembly today instead of math, by writing it on the schedule. Half days, field trips, early release, and guest speakers should all be addressed ahead of time. It is when the student doesn't know what's coming next that they become full of anxiety and fear. Even if you think it's obvious what's next, it might not be obvious to them.

RULES

Rules? Yes, rules. Most students with ASD are described as "rule-bound." I can explain why, but let's just get right to how you can use this to your advantage. Put all rules in writing. The printed rules seem to hold some magical influence… once it's written down, it's a rule that must be followed. This has been a steadfast rule that has worked for most of the kids I've worked with, especially students who can read. They must follow the schedule. They stop when the timer goes off, and they follow the rules. The key here is to make sure *your* rules are also *their* rules. A lot of the time the student has his own hidden set of rules. Maybe cabinet doors need to be shut, math has to end at 1:55, and they can't use a pen, only a pencil. Try to find out what their rules are to avoid meltdowns and work around them. WRITE DOWN THE RULES! With students who are very verbal and disruptive, writing on a sticky note, "be quiet" and putting it on his desk will work. This is also why social stories work so well.

What are social stories?

Social stories were created by Carol Gray in 1991, to help teach social skills to people with autism spectrum disorders. They are a short description of a situation, activity, or even problem, which includes specific information about what to expect in that situation. For a younger child, we are going on a field trip… you put in pictures of the bus, you describe where you're going and when with pictures to support it, where or how you will eat lunch when you return. A short example is in Figure 18.

Figure 18: *Social Story Example*

Note: *Kurtzman, S. (2020). Storyboard that [Photograph]. https://www. storyboardthat.com/articles/e/social-story-examples*

Remember… no surprises! Predictability and knowing what's next relieves the anxiety. For a High School student the story may describe the assembly when you are going and what's after the assembly. Any changes in routine, like assemblies, fire drills, lockdowns, guest speakers, rainy day schedules, a classroom party, a high school dance, etc. would be deserving of a social story.

Parents typically create social stories for the first day of school with pictures of the school and the teacher, what time lunch is, and where lunch will be. You'd be surprised how much prep the parent of a child with Autism has put into getting ready for the first day of school, including multiple visits to the school and playground. To the best of your ability, communicate to that parent your schedule prior to the first day of school. Then the parent can get that communicated to the child through social stories.

I also like to use social stories to curb some negative behaviors with pictures of the child doing the positive behavior and how happy that makes me and his family.

HIDDEN RULES

Society itself has a bunch of obscure rules for a very concrete, literal person to handle. In the popular book *The Hidden Curriculum: Practical Solutions For Understanding Unstated Rules In Social Situations,* the writers brought attention to the unspoken, unwritten rules and beliefs that influence how people interact with each other in life and how students on the autism spectrum remain unaware of those hidden rules (Myles et al., 2004). Neurotypical students can use observational learning to build their social accomplishments by understanding the subtle rules and expectations embedded into social situations. The hidden curriculum includes everything learned that was not directly taught. It consists of the unwritten rules and expectations that were intuited from the social environment.

There are many examples of hidden rules such as whispering in a library, not pulling pants all the way down at the urinal, or what to wear to a party.

She included scenarios like what to do if you get a gift that you don't like, what if you get a splinter or a nosebleed, and how to keep yourself busy in the car. But the whole idea of our hidden rules in our society is lost on our students with Autism. For instance, in the boy's/men's bathroom, there are rules. When a man is at a urinal when you walk in, you do not use the urinal next to him. You skip a urinal or go to the one that is furthest away. You don't pull your pants all the way down at a urinal. Us moms and female teachers might not have ever thought to prep a young man for that. But I had a student who pulled his pants all the way down and other kids would smack his naked butt. Some of these rules are really important to learn. He had no idea why they were smacking him. A social story reviewing these rules helped him and gave him a choice to go in the stall and shut the door or only unzip his fly, keeping his pants up. There are rules in the grocery store. You keep your cart on your side and don't block the aisle. (Recently single men don't seem to know this rule). But seriously, isn't it annoying when someone blocks the aisle and doesn't see you and keeps reading the label? I want to bash my cart into them and then say excuse me... but that would not be what we do in the grocery store, would it? Basically, be aware that there are hidden rules that all of the other students understand and your student with ASD will not. It seems prevalent with what's fashionable and good hygiene like wearing deodorant.

BEHAVIOR

When things don't go as the student expected them to, or if he is overwhelmed, you may see undesirable behaviors such as screaming, yelling, hitting, throwing items or chairs, pulling out hair, and banging his head. ***Are you kidding me? Fudge nuggets!*** I know you're scared. It's ok because you will understand it. Behavior always comes down to, excessive anxiety, the inability to process sensory input, poor communication skills, poor motor planning, or the need for repetitive, predictable activities.

When a child has a challenging behavior, I always ask **"What is he trying to tell me?** Did I break one of his rules? **Did I make sure to follow the three rules of work?**

1. What is the work he has to do?
2. How much work does he have to do?
3. What is the next activity?

It could be that 25 math problems on the sheet are too much or that you or the paraprofessional are overcueing them and they have to reprocess information every time. For instance, if you say,

"Write your name on the paper" and the student needs three seconds to process, and after two seconds, you prompt again, "Write your name on the paper"… he has to process that all over again.

Students with Autism often have difficulty **tolerating mistakes**. When they hear that they got a problem wrong or that they need to do it over again… they may instantly melt down. It's part of having a low frustration tolerance. Some ways to help them with their fear of it being too hard or too much is to start an activity for them, provide hurdle help (help when they are stuck), or I'll do a problem, you do a problem. We've talked about not presenting too much at one time. If you want to avoid the anxiety-riddled meltdown from him being overwhelmed, then be sure to take the extra minute to cross out problems they don't need to do, rip the paper in half, or highlight just a few problems for them to do. It also really helps avoid behaviors by keeping structure in the classroom with consistent ways of presenting information.

Did I give him good, **concrete, clear, and precise directions**? Confusing directions are saying things like "get busy" "have nice hands" or "knock it off." That doesn't make sense to a person that takes things literally……. 'What about my hands?" "Knock what off?"

Also… don't say "don't"! ***What? You just said don't say don't.*** I did. If you say, "Don't run," "don't pick your nose," Don't hit," or "Don't bite"….What is the last word you hear? That may be the only word that the student heard and it accelerates the behavior. So say what you want the student to do:

Put your hands on the desk.

Walk!

Pick up your pencil.

Start problem 3.

Hands down.

Quiet.

Students with ASD can be incredibly disruptive when overstimulated, overwhelmed, and anxious during transitions and unexpected situations. A good rule of thumb is for teachers to consider negative behavior from students with autism as **communication**. Students with ASD may be trying to communicate their wants, needs, anxieties, and frustrations in the only way they know how. These behaviors may include:

- Rocking
- Fidgeting
- Tapping
- Humming
- Yelling
- Mimicking sounds and words
- Laughing out loud
- Out-of-seat behavior
- Stimming
- Interrupting
- Calling out
- Arguing
- Refusing
- Aggressions: hitting, biting, spitting, pulling hair, throwing chairs, property destruction
- Running out of the classroom

It is important to remember that students with autism almost always have a communication disorder. The very diagnosis of autism is severe deficits in communication and social interaction, with restricted interests and repetitive behaviors, usually with sensory processing deficits and differences. Prevention is key. Although all behavior should be seen as communication, it does not mean that all behavior is acceptable. Students with autism should be included, valued, and provided accommodations, services, and support to address their specific needs and disabilities. However, they do not have the right to disrupt the learning of others. When classroom behavior interferes with the safety and learning of others, the IEP team comes together to determine if a personalized behavior plan is needed. A functional behavior analysis is performed when deemed necessary, and a behavior plan is created. The most common areas of difficulty are transitions, work assignments, recess, and unstructured "down" time.

TRANSITIONS

Transitions are the end of one activity before starting another when a child must stop one activity and start another. When required to stop an activity, the student must demonstrate flexible thinking and shift thoughts and attention from one activity to what will come next. As students with autism typically demonstrate executive functioning issues, this is not always possible for them to do, especially when they are not finished with the assignment or project and time is up. Students on the autism spectrum have a greater need for predictability as they have difficulty understanding what will come next without a consistent, predictable classroom routine. Transitions are often difficult for students with autism as they frequently rely on routines to traverse social situations, such as knowing what comes next, what is expected, and what the rules are. When there are changes to the routine, it can be overwhelming as the student with ASD cannot typically predict other people's behavior, understand unwritten rules, and shift attention quickly. Ways to reduce anxiety and create smoother transitions:

1. Give advanced notice. "You have 5 more minutes until it is time for art." Giving a warning can help the brain get

ready to shift gears and relieve anxiety rather than abruptly announcing, "It is time for art; pack up."

2. Use visual supports. Visual supports such as timers, schedules, first-then boards, and transition cards.

3. Use structure and consistency. A consistent and structured schedule can help make the transitions more automatic, reducing the amount of work the brain needs.

4. Use reduced language.

PEOPLE FIRST LANGUAGE

Huh? People First Language is a term used to respectfully put the person before their disability. You may be thinking, "Oh here we go with the politically correct version of talking. ***No, I was not thinking that. But I don't think I understand how to do it. I don't want to say the wrong thing to my students or their parents.*** O.k., It's a simple rule to put the person first. Students with disabilities are most importantly students, people, and individuals. They have a variety of interests and needs just like typically developing students do. A student with a disability is more *like* other students than they are different. The disability is just a challenge or a medical diagnosis. We don't describe what we consider a typical student with asthma as our "asthmatic student." We also don't describe our student with Autism as our "Autistic student."

Figure 19: *People First Language Guidelines*

PEOPLE-FIRST LANGUAGE

Everyone deserves dignity and respect. Yet historically, our words have contributed to negative attitudes and misrepresentations about the value of people with disabilities in our society. To end discrimination — at work, at school, and in our communities — it's important to stop using language that denies a person's value, individuality, and capability. As its name implies, People-First Language puts the individual first and the disability second. It's an objective way to refer to people with disabilities. By focusing on the person rather than the disability, it aims to end harmful generalizations, assumptions, and stereotypes.

When referring to people with disabilities, be considerate with your words. Don't use terms that disrespect or devalue. Some people will want you to use People-First Language. Some will prefer you use Identity-First Language, which embraces a person's disability as an identity and puts the identifying word first ("autistic person" instead of "person with autism"). Others may not want you to mention their disability at all. **Always ask.** The following chart includes examples of People-First Language. Find more examples at www.tcdd.texas.gov.

Use this:	Instead of this:
people with disabilities	the handicapped, the disabled
people without disabilities	normal, healthy, whole, or typical people
person with a congenital disability	person with a birth defect
person with Down syndrome	Downs person, mongoloid, mongol
person with quadriplegia, person with paraplegia, person with a physical disability	a quadriplegic, a paraplegic
person of short stature, little person	a dwarf, a midget
person who communicates without speech, person who uses a communication device	dumb, mute
person with a learning disability	learning disabled
person with a mental health condition	crazy, insane, psycho, mentally ill, emotionally disturbed
person with an intellectual or developmental disability	mentally retarded, retarded, slow, idiot, moron
person who uses a wheelchair	confined to a wheelchair, wheelchair-bound

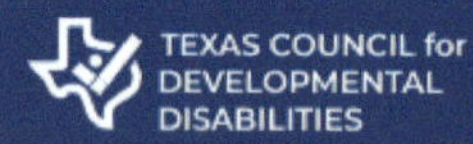

Note: *Texas Council for Developmental Disabilities (n.d.) People First Language [PDF]. https://tcddprd1.wpenginepowered.com/wp-content/uploads/2022/08/ People-First- Language-TCDD.pdf*

According to The Arc, http://www.thearc.org/who-we-are/media-center/people-first-language over 54 million Americans have a disability. One in five students in your classroom probably has a disability. The Centers for Disease Control's Autism and Developmental Disabilities Monitoring (ADDM) reported that "approximately 1 in 36 children in the United States have been identified with an Autism Spectrum Disorder (ASD)." It's so interesting that in 1980, the incidence of Autism was 1 in 10,000. But that's a whole different conversation.

The language you use in your classroom, in the lunchroom, and in the community to describe students with disabilities, has the power to shape other people's beliefs and ideas about that person. The saying 'sticks and stones can break my bones, but words can never hurt me' is not true. We know this. We know that there are some things people say to you that you never forget. Words are powerful! The old descriptors for students with disabilities perpetuate negative stereotypes and reflect prejudice. In the age of no tolerance for bullying, putting the student first when speaking of him is important to set the tone in your classroom. Just as, if you ignore the student with ASD that comes in for science, the rest of the class will ignore him too. If you make him feel welcome and add the expectation that the rest of the class should greet him or help him when they can, you set a much richer culture in your classroom: One of respect. "When we describe people by their labels of medical diagnoses, (the Down's kid or the Autistic student}, we devalue and disrespect them as individual students. Their disability is not a "problem." I often hear special education teachers describe kids as "a runner," "a stuffer," or "a biter." It's really not appropriate to speak of our students in this manner. Our words create attitudes and influence our feelings and decisions. People-First Language puts the person before the disability. It describes **what** a person has, not **who** a person is.

TALKING TO PARENTS

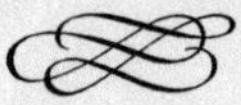

(sigh)

Omg, phone calls to parents are the hardest thing I do all day. I always worry about how it will go. The most important thing for ANY Mom is that they feel that you like their child. Even better if you seem to "love" their kid. If you're a mother or father yourself, you know it's true. The very second that you so much as think that the teacher doesn't like your child, you are ready to go to war. That Mama Bear comes out of you and you can't control yourself! When communicating with a parent of a child on the spectrum, make sure that you convey how much you like their child. You're a teacher… you know you love the kids in your classroom and are concerned about their success or failures. Just simply convey how much you like them. Do not drop a BUT… into the conversation. A parent with a child on the spectrum is just waiting for that to come out of your mouth… so don't do it.

IMPORTANCE OF FAMILY COMMUNICATION

To effectively communicate with parents of a child with autism, it is important to understand what a typical day may look like. Angela Conrad (2017) explained *A Day in our Life with Autism* in a blog on AutismAwarenss.com. Her day is typical of many families with children on the spectrum. She described the routine and consistency needed to avoid meltdowns, the strategic planning needed to do any activities out of the ordinary, watch the same show repeatedly, and eat the same snack, food, and drink every day with a daily trip to McDonald's. She went on to say that sometimes they sleep, sometimes not; her house is full of picture schedules, swings, trampolines, weighted blankets, and vests; she is constantly filling out paperwork for her son and speaking in acronyms (IEP, ABA, ST, OT, PT, LRE, AAC, IDEA) all the time. She finds her son on top of counters and cabinets and is constantly worried he will get out of the house. Some families are not able to go out to dinner, have friends visit, or leave their children with a babysitter. Some students have therapy (i.e., speech, occupational) every evening after school. Other families have it a little easier with fewer meltdowns, a little less structure, and more language from their child. However, most families have structure, limited food preferences, tantrums, and meltdowns in their lives even as their child matures.

Imagine how stressful the day could be:

The child wakes up between 4 and 5 every day because his body does not produce enough serotonin. He will only eat dry Cinnamon Toast Crunch for breakfast, so Mom buys cases at a time. Mom feels hopeful today and introduces another cereal brand which gets dumped on the floor (for mom to clean up), simultaneously inciting a screaming fit. Mom calms her son by giving him her phone, so he will eat his breakfast and stop screaming. After Mom cleans up the mess, she tries to take her phone back, inciting another tantrum. She does not want to give him the iPad because she wants to work on setting up preschool tasks today. She sets the timer and tells him when the timer goes off, the iPad is done, and he can play with toys. Meanwhile, it is time to wake her other two children so they can go to school. She starts making them breakfast, and the timer goes off. She takes the iPad away and gets out a box of Legos, and another tantrum ensues. Mom ignores him and gets the other two ready for school. She drives them to school, so everyone needs to get in the car. Her son will not put his shoes on, but it's cold outside, and she wrestles with him to get them on. He kicks one off on the way to the car. Everyone gets in the car and must listen to Cocomelon, or her son will cry and scream. She drops the other children off at school at 8:30. Mom and son return home, and she lets him watch Cocomelon and Baby Shark and play with Legos while she starts the laundry and cleans the kitchen. The Baby Shark show ends, and he brings her the remote and whines. She models for him to sign and say" more" and waits for him to do it. She puts another show on. She sits down and attempts to play with Legos with him, and he starts to cry, grabs all the Legos out of her hands, and throws them. She feels guilty for letting him watch TV and line up his Legos, but she doesn't have the energy to go through another tantrum. She cleans the house and does chores until it is time for lunch. McDonald's chicken nuggets and fries are the only things her child will eat for lunch, and they have to be fresh, so she gets him in the car, not worrying about the shoes this time, and drives to McDonald's. They go home, and he eats his lunch while watching the iPad because it is the only way he will sit at the table. It is time for speech therapy, and mom gets him ready by taking him potty, making him sit for three minutes, and changing his pullup. She has to wrestle with him to brush his teeth while he cries and screams. Mom picks up the Legos and puts the couch back together to prepare for the speech therapist. The therapist arrives, and the mom sits on the floor and plays with the therapist and her son, trying to learn what she should be doing to increase his ability to communicate. The therapist leaves, and Mom continues with some puzzles on the floor and works on colors and signing with her son. She tries to snuggle with him and read him a book, but he pulls away, whining, and he tries to rip the book. It is time to go pick up her other kids from school, and her son throws himself down, saying "No, no." She tells him, "I will give you candy if you get up and come get in the car." He stops crying, walks barefoot to the car, and eats his candy. They pick up the kids from school, listening to Cocomelon the entire time "Baby shark do, do, do…" The family returns home, and she gives her son the iPad and a bowl of chips so that she can help her other two children with their homework. They finish their homework, go to their room, and Mom starts cooking dinner. She makes dinner for the family and a separate mac and cheese dinner for her son. She chops up one small piece of broccoli in the mac and cheese. The family sits down to dinner, and her son runs around the table. He looks at the mac and cheese and leaves the table. Dad gets up and goes and gets his son and tells him to sit down at the table and eat his mac and cheese. He starts crying and yelling, and nobody else at the table can talk. Mom figured this would happen and gave him another bowl of mac and cheese without the broccoli, but it was too late, and the mac and cheese was ruined. Mom gives her son the iPad and a bowlful of crackers and lets him leave the table. Now the other two children are done with dinner and asking to be excused, but Mom wants to talk about their day. They talk for a few minutes, and Mom eats her cold food while everyone else leaves the table. Mom asks if Dad will bathe their son and brush his teeth because she is tired. Dad reminds Mom that he worked all day while she got to stay home, but he will do it. Mom does the dishes and helps the other two kids get ready for bed. She hears screaming from the other bathroom and assumes Dad is working on toothbrushing with their son. She relieves Dad and helps her son get his pajamas on. The occupational therapist told Mom that she wants him to start dressing himself. She gets his pajamas and tells him to put them on. He runs around the room and jumps on his bed naked, ignoring Mom. Mom yells at him to get his jammies on. He continues to jump on the bed. She blocks the doorway because she does not want him to get out and run around the house. She tells him after he gets his jammies on, he can watch Cocomelon. She hands him his pajama bottoms, and he drops them and runs back to jump on his bed. Mom gives up, feels guilty, and wrestles with him to get his pajamas on. He continues to jump on his bed, and she turns on Cocomelon. Mom gets herself ready for bed even though it is only 8:30. She stops in to say goodnight to her other two kids. Her eldest reminds her that he has a project after school tomorrow. She puts herself to bed and hears her son in the pantry. She has to decide if she needs to go get him out of the pantry. She decides to get up and go get him. He has moved a chair over to reach the Doritos on the top shelf and has eaten half the bag. She takes him back to bed and lays down with him. Mom wakes up and finds her son gone. She wonders what time it is. She lies there and thinks to herself, "I did lock the top of the front door before I went to bed, right?" She doesn't remember locking it, so she gets up frantically, looking for her son.

An important thing for teachers to understand is that most students on the spectrum cannot effectively communicate, especially when they are upset. Even extremely verbal students who talk incessantly and can state every fact about every dinosaur cannot efficiently discuss their day, leaving out the important parts such as they have a test tomorrow, or another child ate half of his lunch. The executive functioning and communication deficits previously discussed interfere with their ability to state a succinct summary and pull out the pertinent details. Many students struggle to answer complex questions such as why and how. Imagine a Mom picking up her child from school. She gives him a warm greeting, and he slumps down in his seat and turns away. Mom asks, "What happened? Why are you upset?" The student does not and cannot answer.

Parent-teacher communication is essential for the student with autism. Envision trying to talk with a nonverbal child about their day when there is limited information available. "I know you had art today." "Did you color?" "Paint?" "Glue?" "Let me look in your backpack." "Oh, you have a picture." "Did you make this today?" "Did you make it last week?" "Did you make this in art?" "It's beautiful! I love it." Incomplete information makes it virtually impossible to talk with a nonverbal child about their day. It results in a series of guesses and often highlights the wrong information, reinforcing the wrong communication skills. Although a teacher cannot communicate every event of the day to the parent, steps can be put in place to provide the most information possible.

Crissy Kelly (2020) wrote an article in The Autism Helper that included tips for teachers to communicate with parents. When corresponding with parents, teachers should proactively set and share clear boundaries from the start. Many teachers have found a welcome letter effective in sharing information about the classroom, the teacher's background and interests, and the best communication methods for the teacher. Making the parents feel just as welcome as the students is important. Sharing good news with parents is a good strategy for building positive relationships as well as including details such as, "Johnny played in the sand with a general education peer today for over ten minutes, and they were both laughing!" Another great tip is to discuss the antecedent, behavior, and consequence when discussing a negative situation. This allows the teacher to state facts and demonstrates to the parents that they understand the situation. For example, compare the two statements: "Johnny made poor choices today. He had difficulty sitting in science group and pushed another student," versus "Johnny was sitting in science group today and may have been uncomfortable with peers too close to him. He pushed another student, so we discussed better options than pushing and made a seating adjustment so that he had more space." The later statement reflects that the teacher understood what caused the behavior and was able to fix it. For more ways to effectively communicate with parents, see Table 1. Another strategy is to give a compliment sandwich. The teacher starts with a compliment about the student, followed by concern. It is helpful to state the behavior that the teacher wants, such as "turning in work" or "raising their hand," versus addressing what is not wanted, such as to "stop calling out" or "not completing assignments." The conversation ends on a positive note with another compliment. The conversation may look like this:

"Hi, Mrs. Jones. Jeremy really loved our science unit this week. He has been doing so well with working in a group and performing the experiments (1st compliment/top bun). "I like to call on the students to tell me about their current process. Jeremy often answers for the other students, so I have been sure to call each student by name when asking my questions" (concern/meat). "I have talked to Jeremy about only calling out when I call him by name. Should we make a social story? Can you talk with him about this?"

"Thank you for your help with this. He is a complete rock star in science, and I love having him in my class" (2nd compliment/bottom bun).

Table 1: *How to Effectively Communicate with Parents*

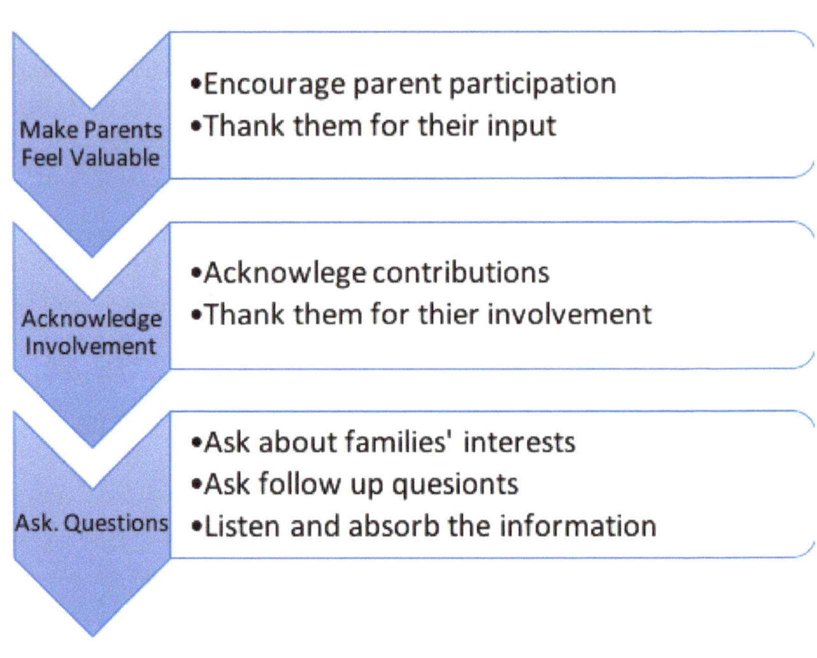

Note: *Walden University (2022).* Nine ways to improve parent-teacher communication. *https://www.waldenu.edu/online-bachelors-programs/bs-in-elementary- education/resource/nine-ways-to-improve-parent-teacher-communication*

We are going to play "Let's imagine"…..Imagine your child doesn't like hugs from you or touches. Your child doesn't call you mama, or mommy, and doesn't tell you he loves you. Imagine preschools calling to tell you your child bit somebody again, so you need to find another preschool. Imagine a speech therapist telling you she can't work with your child because he's too difficult. Imagine your child screaming through the whole bedtime routine of taking a bath, brushing teeth, and reading a book. Imagine a school calling every other day to tell you that your child hit someone. Imagine going to a meeting every year with 6 or 7 people on the other side of the table and just trying to advocate for what's best for your child and listen to people speak in acronyms and technical jargon that you are trying to navigate. Imagine sitting in these IEP meetings and the general education teacher is telling you why your child doesn't belong in her class. Imagine your child breaking your t.v., or your grandmother's vase in a fit of uncontrollable rage. Imagine having to cook your child chicken nuggets or waffles every night, because it's the only thing you can get him to eat. Imagine your child never being invited to birthday parties. Imagine never being able to have a babysitter. Imagine being held hostage by fear of an extreme meltdown that you are just too tired to deal with.

So like I said…..Don't judge. Don't ever judge. The proverb, "Before you criticize a man, walk a mile in his shoes" is very accurate. If you have not lived on that island, you don't know what it is like. You are going to find yourself in a position as the teacher, to help the paraprofessionals or even therapists not judge the parent.

"You never really know a man until you understand things from his point of view *until you climb into his skin and walk around in it."* -Atticus Finch

Harper Lee, To Kill a Mockingbird. J.B. Lippincott & Co., 1960

Well, that makes me want to call home….

On the other side of the coin, once you've established a communication system where mom knows what's going on during the day and knows what homework to work on you can set boundaries. You don't need to spend hours communicating with this parent; that is unreasonable. But you may come across it. I can tell you from experience and being burnt several times, that the parent that you "bend over backward for" is also the parent that will "stick it to you" in the end. Some parents have fought for so long, they don't know how to stop fighting. So communicate positively with Mom and set boundaries.

AFTERWORD

This was a lot of information to take in. Knowing this information will make all of the difference in understanding autism. The biggest takeaways from this book should be:

Behavior is communication. The student is telling you something. What are they telling you?

Prepare for transitions. Use timers, warnings, and visual cues.

Avoid too much stimulation/distractions.

Set the tone for your class with a welcoming, inclusive attitude.

When presenting work make sure these questions are answered:

Did I make sure to follow the three rules of work?

1. What is the work I have to do?
2. How much work do I have to do?
3. What is the next activity?

I wish you the best of luck! I know you will do great because you already made the effort to learn more. I'm proud of you!

Sincerely,

Dr. Teri Baldwin

If you require more support for feeding or speech and language services there is information on my website:

www.speechblossoms.net

There is information about life skills on our school website:

www.thepassagelearningforlife.com

You can purchase my in-depth textbook that includes everything there is to know about autism and treatment strategies.

Understanding Autism: Treating the Whole Child